Table of Contents

2. 3. Introduction to China: Strategic Thinking and Its Concepts of Order

China called itself Zhongguo which means "the Middle Kingdom" or "the central states" which is the explained as the center of the civilized world. However, there are two explanations on the meaning. First, the "middle Kingdom" means that China is the central state of the civilized world which surrounded by the barbarians or tributary states. The emperors of the Middle Kingdom were the heaven mandates which sent to pacify the great harmony on earth. The second, the Zhongguo was used by Chou empire which was dated 1000 BC that ruled North China plain which regarded itself as the middle of the planet.

The middle Kingdom is one of the greatest and oldest civilizations of the world which had a strong influence and spread over the continents. The cultures, wisdoms, the population, military, and land size has had given China the superiority to neighboring states, and those ideas has been spreading and accepting worldwide. In its 5000 years history, China has been going under the splendid and worse time which in the combinations of these lessons, China has enough experiences that enabled it to goes on their own way. As A People' daily commented:

With its unique road, unique theory, unique institutions and unique culture, the Chinese road that has been enriched and developed by Xi Jinping's New Era Socialism with Chinese Characteristics transcends "Western centrism" and greatly stimulates development of the broad range of developing countries' self-confidence in "going their own way."

China views history as the unstoppable flow. Therefore, Looking at the past, China feel proud and humiliated, joyful and painful, as well as worry. Joyfulness and proud were on its great magnificent cultures and philosophies that were the preeminent. Chinese emperors felt that they were sent by the heaven to rule the earth, but not by conquered rather than by purifying its magnificent cultures and let others who wanted to be prosperous come to seek them and recognize the power of emperors. When it sent the envoy to other states it was the celestial envoy, but when receiving others it felt that the emperor summoned the barbarians and sometimes the envoys were baited with different ways. One more, Chinese wisdom and insight are the most important. There were many prominent philosophers and strategic thinkers which has been guiding China and the world such as Lao Zi, Confucius, Mencius, Zhuang Zi, Mozi, Sun Tzu and many others. In addition, the

Chinese people are another over-powerful force. Chinese leaders have the confidence in their people as the industrious, hard work, brave, intelligent, persistent, and self-determined.

Throughout the history, all the people struggled to survive by themselves in the times of wars, natural disasters, famine, civil wars, world wars, and so on. In the time of the hundred schools of thoughts, the warring states, and during Han dynasty and so on the ideas were developed profoundly. In Song Dynasty 960 was a great time of Chinese civilization development, highly economic growth and revolutions, technological advancement and invention. The printing, banknotes, gunpowder were invented during this period. The naval power and naval navigation in central Asia, Africa, and almost throughout the world was first come to exist. The economic growth was the most remarkable by developing the exchange trade with foreign countries, urbanization, and agricultural revolution which lead to high growth population. These factors contributed to the global civilization and development. As president Xi Jinping addressed:

During the civilization and development process of more than 5,000 years, the Chinese nation has made an indelible contribution to the civilization and advancement of mankind.

China also feels concern when looking back at the past. There was no dynasty in the imperial China that longer more than 400 years. Henry Kissinger noted in the Romance of Three Kingdoms "after long time of division, united, and after long time of unity, divided". In poem China was also named **"Jiuzhou"** "Nine Regions". It was supposed to be divided into nine regions. Its present condition of different regions such as Xijiang, Tibet, Taiwan, and Hong Kong with the historical perspective is the great concern to Communist Party. Probably this is the reason that Chinese leaders on one hand control the military strictly and another hand trying to satisfy people by economic development and anti-corruption campaign. Xi Jinping said "the collapse of Soviet Union was that the party did not hold the military, so the Communist must stand firm on military leadership". Another reason is that China is building on the premise that "as long as the economy still grow and people can enjoy a better lives, they will tolerate with many things". Deng said "the force would end the unrest but only economic reform could prevent it in the future, an idea that was unpopular then but has since shaped china as it is today". George Friedman wrote in his book "The Next 100 Years: A Forecast for the 21st Century" that "China is held together by money". While Charles Patrick Fitzgerald wrote "the Chinese are less a nation than a fusion of peoples united by a common culture, and the history of China is the record of an expanding culture".

China was humiliated, conquered, and destructed throughout late 19th century until mid-20th. The senior was conquered by a lower. The Japanese invasions, the opium wars, and the colonization of the western were the great painful of Chinese people and leaders. The three "alls" Japanese policy was the most bitterly suffered and destroyed, "Kill all", "burn all", "and loot all". China was a senior and a preeminent but was humiliated by the barbarians. Resulting from these agonies is the temptation to use it as the nationalism and strategic rethinking of rebuilding China. The Communist Party uses it to consolidate people, to show the shared enemy, and strengthen the military might. The victory anniversary is held annually to remind the historical pain. The Chinese strategic actions in present are also can be understood by weaknesses that was defeated. They concluded that "the defeat was not cause by military strategy, but the outdated system, the lower equipment and the ignorance of maritime strategy". Therefore, China now orients its military strategy toward maritime, strict training and discipline, and modernizes the equipment. China accessibility to the seas also is facing the Challenges by the US naval, Japanese, South Korean, India, and with some of Asean members. Deng Xiaoping advised before leaving office:

"Enemy troops are outside the wall. They are stronger than we. We should be mainly on the defensive".

With the proud and pain of the past and the present condition, China strategic actions that designed in the present day desire to be the center of the global power in the future. In order to understand China more, let go through the evolution of the seven China. David Kelly observed the development of China and categorized into seven stages which he calls "Seven Chinas".

1. China as the Sufficient Civilization: Henry Kissinger believes that the culture is the exceptional value of China which is used to put the world under the value "great harmony to all under the heaven".

2. China as the most Humiliated Nation: China believes that it is the senior, the heaven candidates that was conquered and despised by the barbarian. The great and longest history of civilization that was full of proud was looked down bitterly and forced to abandoned and

accepted the others. Xi Jinping said ""After the Opium War, China has been repeatedly defeated by countries which were smaller and less populous. Kowloon and the New Territories were then forced to leave China's embrace at that time, (and) China's history was full of the nation's humiliation and the people's sorrow."

3. The Leader of the Developing World: among the late developer, we lead. The competitions between the US and Soviet in the Cold War divided the world into two blocs. There was Africo-Asian conference in Bandung aimed at promoting economic and cultural cooperation and opposed to the colonialism or neocolonialism. The conference led to the non-alignment movement. China since then and until nowadays has the intention to lead them, and become the global leader at the end. Addressed to the UN, Deng show the intention to oppose the two superpowers and want to lead the developing world "The whole world is in turbulence and unrest. The situation is one of "great disorder under heaven," as we Chinese put it. This "disorder" is a manifestation of the sharpening of all the basic contradictions in the contemporary world. It is

accelerating the disintegration and decline of the decadent reactionary forces and stimulating the awakening and growth of the new emerging forces of the people".

4. China as the Champion of Plurality: *We end the era of the western and American hegemony.* The western ruled the world from the 18th to the late of 20th through colonialism. After the Second World War the world was led by bilateral superpowers, US and Soviet. The Collapse of the Soviet, the world led by only one superpower, a unilateral power US. Through its comprehensive national power, cooperation with various organizations, and the creation of various networks, as well as the rising of major powers, China is the best one that drawing the world to "multilateralism".

5. China as the Sovereign Survivor: *leave us to survive as the communist power.* The communist that was originated in Russia and them brought to establish in China was no longer survive in its homeland, but China. It survive through, different means, reform and opening up, and the adaptation of the name "Socialism with

Chinese Characteristics, and Socialism with Chinese Characteristics in New Era". Beyond surviving is going to have influence. The Tiananmen Square event was the most threat to the survival of Communist but also the opportunity to "survive for long times". Deng said "we could benefit from this incident".

6. China as the Last Man Standing: the west is in decline, while we have deep pocket. In the Moa' Era China economy was very bad through the continuous revolutions. Deng then focused on the economic development "to be rich is Glorious". The two systems, reform and opening up, and the state-enterprises help China grows rapidly and suffered little from the 2008 global economic crisis.

7. China as the Herald of The High Frontier: we share and safeguard the global commons. Xi Jinping declared China enters the New Era and promises to take more responsibility, support the UN, proposed the new type of major powers relations, and proposed the ideas of the community of shared future of mankind.

With the proud and the painful in history, the present conditions, and the ambition to be the global power, China has designed the Grand Strategy of what it calls "Comprehensive National Power". China has to be stronger in all dimensions: economy, military, diplomacy, cultural and technological advancement in order to stand as the global power. That is going to be prosperous, cultural advancement, civilized, and democratic China. Then, as the power grows, its influence and power will be recognized. However, there are some challenges that pose to prevent China such as US and its allies, Geopolitics, economic stability, and its internal issues.

2.3.1 China's strategic Intentional Interpretation

The People's Republic of China was established in 1949 when the communist party led by Chairman Mao and Zhou Enlai as the premier. The first generation of china was the struggling to purify and unify the whole nation through continuous revolutions. The first generation faced the domestic and external challenges. Domestically, the continuous revolutions, and Great Leap Forward, as well as just emerged from the world wars, and civil wars, China was heavily destructed socially, politically, and economically. Internationally, China faced the difficulty in managing the relationship between US and Soviet. The US encirclement from

Korean Peninsula to Taiwan until Vietnam in which triggered China to entered into the Korean War in 1950s, and supported the Vietnamese war against US. It also faced the nuclear threat from Soviet on the border and ideological issues in 1960s. However, the main objectives were: Purify and strengthening the ideologies and cultures, and the unification of the whole country. In 1957 Moa said:

> *"The unification of our country, the unity of our people and the unity of our various nationalities - these are the basic guarantees of the sure triumph of our cause".*
> *"Communists should set an example in being practical as well as far-sighted. For only by being practical can they fulfil the appointed tasks, and only far-sightedness can prevent them from losing their bearings in the march forward."*

The Second Generation

Deng Xiaoping is recognized as the paramount leader of the second generation until his resignation in 1992. Unlike Moa, the second generation focused on the economic development and the pioneering to economic reform. Deng, who went to France in his early age and then to Moscow, praised about the development of the west and felt of the backwardness of his society. Therefore, the objectives were: architect the combination socialist ideology with the pragmatic economy which called "Socialism with Chinese Characteristics". Deng who came to power amidst the social and economic destruction wanted to develop the economy in order to solve other issues "to be rich is glorious". He reformed and opened up the country to the global market and foreign investment which brought Chinese economic fast-growth. The schools were reopened and sent the students and officers to learn abroad. In his time, even though the US-China relations were normalized, he faced the democratic movement that he said "initiated by other" referred to US in order to stagnate the economic reform. He also went to war to force Vietnam who invaded Cambodia to withdraw in 1989, and cooperated with US supported the Afghan against Soviet. During these period, China played important roles in leading the developing countries, but also concerned and needed more times to growth. Deng advised:

> "Observe carefully, secure our position, cope with affairs calmly, hide our capacities and bide our time, be good at maintaining a low profile, and never claim leadership." "

Third Generation

Jiang Zemin was a core leader of third generation from 1992-2002. The generation was looking for continuing economic development by calling for more cooperation and integrated with World Trade Organization. In his addressed to UN general assembly he asked for joining to build up " a brighter world", "respecting others' independence and sovereignty", "build up the common security" and " promoting of multipolar international system".

> "The Chinese people, going all out for the socialist modernization drive, are ready to work with the people of other countries to usher in a better new century".

Domestically, he initiated a socio-political theory which is called "Three Represents". The three represents are: Represents advanced social productive forces which is stands for economic production, Represents the progressive course of China's advanced culture which stands for cultural development, and Represents the fundamental interests of the majority" stands for political consensus.

The Fourth Generation

The generation started from 2002-2012 which the core leaders were Hu Jintao, Wu Bangguo, and Wen Jiabao and so on. Their leadership was a technocratic style and less centralized on political power. The Generation was looking for strengthening its economic growth and social harmony, and multi-cooperation and common development goals. Hu Jintao also proposed for building the harmonious world, strengthening cooperation and coordination for well-rounded development for all countries. Wen Jiabao also called for jointly effort to realize the Millennium Development Goals. The main political objectives were scientific development concept which aimed at guiding socio-economic development toward harmonious society which was incorporated with scientific socialism, sustainable development, social welfare, a humanistic society, increased democracy, and mixing with maxims to the China reality, and the methodology of development. It started to build the major elements of economic advancement and looking forward to catch up high technological and innovative driving. Compared to the west, China is far behind in these fields in which it is very often complained for abusing the intellectual and copy rights.

The Fifth Generation

From the Second Generation to fourth Generation was the time of Socialism with Chinese Characteristics in which was oriented by Deng's advised "hide our capacities and bide our time". What it needed the most were self-preparation, self-strengthening and integrated itself to the world with less responsibility. The Fifth Generation is trying to combine the some key points of the previous leaders and deepening multi-cooperation and expanding its influence to the world and set up the plan to lead the global world. Xi Jinping who came to power in 2012 and was enabled to rule China for whole life is leading China into the very important stage of the global power. The comprehensive National Power has been developing dramatically.. Politically, Xi consolidates the power, sets the Chinese dream of great national rejuvenation, anti-corruption campaign, and mixing political ideologies of the Marxism, Maoism, Deng' thought, three Represents and his thought. Economically, Xi focuses on deeper reform and wider opening up, capacity to catch up the advanced hi-tech, and orients China to focus on local consuming. In short, Xi orients toward the prosperous, cultural advanced, civilized, and democratic China. Internationally, China proposed the Belt and Road Initiative,

New Type of Major Power Relations, the Community of Shared Future, Win-Win cooperation, the New Banks that give Direct Financial Investment, and commitment to uphold international order is drawing China to the more important role ever before and moving China closer to the center of Global World. Xi declared "Socialism with Chinese Characteristics in New Era" "China enters the New Era" which means China is stronger and more confident in "economy, military, politics, diplomacy, technological capacity, and cultural influence".

2.3.2 The Nature of Chinese Strategic Thinking

There are many scholars, politicians and strategists who think about "Chinese Strategic thinking" or in the very common word "what does China want and do?" The world has playing very close attention to China because of its fast growth and its activities inside the and outside China. There are various different views about China's intentional activities. However, In order to get a better understanding, we have to gather those interpretations on China's intention and analysis them. We also have to understand the Chinese' ancient thoughts and philosophies, China's present condition and its future goals. There are great thinkers such as former secretary of state Henry

Kissinger, Lee Kuan Yew, Zbigniew Brzezinski, Kevin Rudd, and Granham Allison and others thinkers.

2.3.2.1 Henry Kissinger's Interpretation of Chinese strategic Thinking

It seems that there is not greater thinker that understands China better than Henry Kissinger. He is an elder statesman, a political scientist, a strategic thinker, a diplomat and a geo-political consultant. He has played the very imminent roles in international politics. He spends all his energy, thoughts and life on the global politics, and the initiator of Sino-US relations. Henry has engaged with Chinese leaders since the first generation of Mao until now. He is the master of Sino-US relations story since the time of Mao. Henry is the most experienced on politics.

Henry Kissinger wrote a very great book "On China". The book elaborates the nature of Chinese strategic thinking in the very lengthy on the major fields. However, it was summarized to understand China as "China prefers to seek and build superior force, psychological domination rather that to confront and engage in conflict directly. It always focuses on the long-term, supremacy, subtlety, indirection, and patient to formulate the relative advantage". The ancient Chinese strategic and military thinker Sun Tzu said "The supreme art of war is to subdue enemy without fighting". The nature of strategy that is looking for building the advantaged and superior positions is now transforming to the "Comprehensive national power" which is seeking to empower China in all dimensions. Sun also taught to "avoid the strengths, attack the weakness of enemy", "appear where we are not expected, and attack where they do not defend". It poses two perspectives: avoid the direct confrontation, and do beyond the expectation". "First, attack the strategy, second, attack the allies, and then attack the enemy to seek quick victory", Sun added. In the Art of War, Sun Tsu said "the art of war is of crucial importance to existence of the State, the matter of life and death, the road to safety and ruin". Therefore, it must be constantly calculated and compared the five factors to determine the military conditions are: (1) The Moral Law; (2) the climate (seasons), (3) Earth (geopolitics); (4) The Commander; (5) Method and discipline. He even on to elaborate that "he knows the victory before the war going to be fought" by calculating these elements:

(1) Which of the two sovereigns is imbued with the Moral Law?

(2) Which of the two generals has most ability?

(3) With whom lie the advantages derived from Heaven and Earth?

(4) On which side is discipline most rigorously enforced?

(5) Which army is stronger?

(6) On which side are officers and men more highly trained?

(7) In which army is there the greater constancy both in reward and punishment?

Henry Kissinger addressed the Chinese intellectual game which represents Chinese strategic approaches. The Game GO or Chinese calls "Weiqi" is the "the game of surrounding pieces" which the player do not seek to confront the enemy or seek total victory, but focus on "the strategic encirclement". Each of the players has 180 pieces with the empty board of grid nineteen by nineteen lines. Contrast to the Chess that all pieces are on the board and confront each other that allow the players to calculate, the Weiqi pieces are not on the board which the player has to use "strategic analysis". He said "The players take turns placing stones at any point on the board, building up positions of strength while working to encircle and capture the opponent's stones. Multiple contests take place simultaneously in different regions of the board. The balance of forces shifts incrementally with each move, as the players implement strategic plans and react to each other's initiatives. Chess is about decisive battle, Weiqi about the protracted campaign. Chess seeks for total victory, single-mindedness, and decisive point, Weiqi seeks for relative advantage, strategic flexibility, and strategic encirclement". He added "Chess is preferred by the west, Weiqi is by Chinese".

In the Book, Henry also mentioned about Chines superior wisdom on how to dealing with the small states and small enemies. That was the ancient wisdom of "using barbarians against the barbarians". To make them exhausted, tired and weak, then force them to subdue to its superiority. He wrote the about China Five Baits which reflect its wisdom, strategy, mature, and subtlety. The baits is the way to influence and control small sates, are:

To give them . . . elaborate clothes and carriages in order to corrupt their eyes; to give them fine food in order to corrupt their mouth; to give them music and women in order to corrupt their ears; to provide them with lofty buildings, granaries and slaves in order to corrupt their stomach . . . and, as for those who come to surrender, the emperor [should] show them favor by honoring them with an imperial reception party in which the emperor should personally serve them wine and food so as to corrupt their mind.

On Chinese uniqueness of cultural and diplomatic influences, henry Kissinger wrote that the American exceptionalism is about its mission of bringing the value of democracy to everywhere of the world. Chinese exceptionalism is cultural. Its cultural magnificence was stretched and influenced most of the part of the world and the oldest over 4000 years. China does want to be like the others, but it has the cultural heir of regarding itself as the Middle Kingdom. The concept of China as the Middle King, he wrote "China graded all other states as various levels of tributaries based on their approximation to Chinese cultural and political forms; in other words, a kind of cultural universality", and it never wanted to control the territory of other states by powers, but by its cultural magnificence and wisdom. In history, the emperors of Middle Kingdom never had the equal relations with other states. They treated those envoys just came to kowtow and recognize the superiority of the Middle Kingdom. China regards herself as the eternal state with the longest history. If others wanted "Chinese wisdom and thought" let they come to seek. In history, especially in Ming Dynasty, China military, innovation, economy, culture, and technology were far away superior to EU at that time.

2.3.2.2 China's Time of Humiliation

In Chapter 3 of his book "On China", he entitled "from the preeminence to decline" the author wrote the unprecedented and historic shock of changing in China history. The historical shift of China from the mandate of heaven in which it graded all states as tributary, to be the equal treatment with Britain and to be the humiliated China was painful. The China concept of International order and relation was changed. He wrote "as the nineteen century progressed, China experienced almost every imaginable shock to its historic image of itself. Before the Opium War, it conceived of diplomacy and international trade mainly as forms of recognition of China's preeminence. Now, even as it entered a period of domestic turmoil, it faced three foreign challenges, any one of which could be enough to overturn a dynasty. These threats came from every direction and in heretofore barely conceivable incarnations". China can draw a better future from this bitter of humiliation and in which it reflects about the Chinese strategic intention. As summarized by Chinese strategic thinkers "our failures did not lie on our man and capacity, but because of our outdated systems, poor equipment and our ignorance of the maritime strategy". These are the reasons that China now focus on its maritime strategy, modernize the weapons and racing to catch up the advanced technology. The author continues that from these periods China reconciled the values that marked its greatness with the technology and commerce on which it would have to base its security.

2.3.2.3 What China Games Over Korean Peninsula?

North Korean Nuclear program is the international concern and threats that would bring the undesirable consequences. In his opening speech to the Senate of Armed Services Committee in 2018, he said "North Korean wants to assure its survival by this nuclear". In his different articles and interviews, he mentions as follows: a) America will lose its creditability of maintaining those countries like Japan and South Korea under its nuclear security, b) The Countries like Japan, South Korean and even Vietnam will follow to build their own nuclear program in which the Nuclear will be widely proliferated, c) China is likely to be risker than US, the world will be under nuclear chaos. But what is China game here? Historically, China used to defend Korea for the invasion of Japan, then Chinese intervention in Korean War in 1950s to end the Chinese period of humiliation and reassert Chinese traditional superiority on the region. There is also about Chinese concept of deterrence which lies on the advantaged positions. In the simple word, China is afraid of encirclement. Henry wrote to the World Street Journal that there are two Chinese major concerns: a) the political and social effects of a North Korean internal crisis on China itself, re-enacting events familiar from millennia of Chinese history, and b) the involving security in Northeast Asia. He also wrote "there are also internal debates in China about whether China prefers a unified Korea or two Koreas". China also thinks about who has more influence on Korea.

2.3.2.4 The South China Sea

The South China Sea is a marginal sea that is part of the Pacific Ocean, encompassing an area from the Karimata and Malacca Straits to the Strait of Taiwan. The sea carries tremendous strategic importance; one-third of the world's shipping passes through it, carrying over $3 trillion in trade each year, it contains lucrative fisheries, which are crucial for the food security of millions in Southeast Asia. Huge oil and gas reserves are believed to lie beneath its seabed. The most important are strategies and shipping straits. The Sea determines Chinese security, power, influence, and economy. As summarized about the China conclusion about its failure that down the Middle Kingdom to the object of colonization was not about its men, but "it was because of outdated system, poor equipment and the ignorance of Maritime strategy". And China concept of deterrence is "advantaged position" and afraid of "encirclement". China is surrounded by many powerful countries on the land borders, internal risky of Tibet and Xinjiang, Japan in long and vast ocean and islands, and the US's navies and ships that can travel closer to China under the word " Free Navigation" and " International Law". Henry ideas are: a) China feels unsecured by American navies because if the war break out, b) America and its allies will move quickly to the land and cities, c) therefore, China has to draw America navies as far as possible, d) China invests tremendous on navy power is coerced by her experienced of bitter invasion and ignorance of Maritime strategy, e) if the war happen, it will use the sea to fight. In the secret negotiation, China says "we guarantee your access to the sea, we do not bloc". America says "no, we do not need your guarantee. It is the free navigation.

We travel under international law". The Sea is the throat of many countries. However, Henry said "He does not much worries about the South China Sea". His most concern is about the "Belt and Road Initiative". The South China Sea "is the security problems. China wants to keep American Navies away from its territory".

2.3.2.5 The Belt and Road Initiative

The Belt and Road Initiative (BRI) is an ambitious effort to improve regional cooperation and connectivity on a trans-continental scale. China stands as the center of world and draws those over 65 countries, maybe expanding to the world and organizations, to connect to the main land China by sharing mutual benefit and consultation. China acts as the bigger, the leader, and the founder who has more money and ideas, and expects to spread its influence over. The BRI aims to strengthening the infrastructure, trade and investment. It covers the most population of the world, 75 percent of energy reserves, and most of them are developing countries. This is what Henry Kissinger concerns the most. He said "it works purely on economy and strategy, nothing to deal with military". "China's

Belt and Road Initiative, in seeking to connect China to Central Asia and eventually to Europe will have the practical significance of shifting the world's center of gravity from the Atlantic to the Pacific and will involve the cultures of Eurasia, each of whom will have to decide what relationship to this region they will see, and so will the United States," Kissinger said. He continued "I am not worry in much in South China Sea. What I am worried the most is the Belt and Road. Nothing can stop because it is not the military plan". He suggested America to join the One Belt One Road.

Therefore, the nature of Chinese strategic thinking is looking for the relative advantages, building up the strength step by carefully step, combining the major elements of power, and using the strategic flexibility through its "Comprehensive National Power". China wants the protracted campaign and bide the time to growth and it can be seen aggressively when its power is strong enough. As Eisenman and Heginbotham wrote in the book *"China Steps Out: Beijing's Major Power Engagement with the Developing World",* that China's foreign policy encompasses major fields of cooperation on "economic interest, diplomatic ties, military and security cooperation, political and cultural ties" all the regions. And when all of these elements growth, the Chinese influence over those regions also does.

2.3.2.6 Henry's Words on China

-Xi Jinping is a tough guy. Xi is saying I would like a peaceful option, but I am going to be ready for another one. He is going to go both roads. He put himself in the strong position to achieve the goal that is difficult to get.

-China is the student of compulsive circumstances. China thinks history is uninterrupted flow. For America, history is the series of achievement.

-China thinks that there is no solution to the problems. Every solution is the admission ticket to another one. For America, every problem has the solution. Therefore, we (America) cut every problem into the segments, and handle in legal criteria that have been planning.

-China thinks in the term of hundred years and conceptually to serve its national interests. US serve its interests by the changing of the term of presidency and pragmatism.

-China needs more time to grow and move the people to the cities, balance the societal classes, and maintain the healthy grow to sustain the communism.

-China exceptionalism is cultural. It uses the Confucius's wisdom and cultural superiority to dominate. America exceptionalism is the value of democracy, human right. We spread to the world by the feeling of missionary.

- When the Chinese court deigned to send envoys abroad, they were not diplomats, but "Heavenly Envoys" from the Celestial Court.

-America has ten issues to fix; China has ten destinations to ask for in the negotiation.

-China produced no religious themes in the Western sense at all. The Chinese never generated a myth of cosmic creation.

-But unlike Machiavelli, Confucius was concerned more with the cultivation of social harmony than with the machinations of power. His themes were the principles of compassionate rule, the performance of correct rituals, and the inculcation of filial piety.

-Where Western strategists reflect on the means to assemble superior power at the decisive point, Sun Tzu addresses the means of building a dominant political and psychological position, such that the outcome of a conflict becomes a foregone conclusion. Western strategists test their maxims by victories in battles; Sun Tzu tests by victories where battles have become unnecessary.

-What will China do? Well, there are two ways. If China goes traditional way, then China will spread its influence gradually as the power grows. And if the differences between US and China get the grid, they will expect that others nations will recognize the fact and act accordingly.

2.3.3 Lee Kuan Yew's Interpretation China's Strategic Thinking

Lee Kuan Yew was a great man with deep-insight whose wisdom was internationally recognized and sought. He was the father of Singapore and brought it from the poorest to the richest country. He increased the Per Capita income from 500 $ to 55,000 $ per year. He made Singapore became the "model society" which focused on the justness, fairness and clean of government, the highly-educated and disciplined citizenship that uphold the responsibility for their destiny, family and national dignity. Singapore became the intellectual and technological center of the regions and has been attractive from the international community.

Lee shared his insight with almost all leaders around the world. The world, especially the US and China, are benefitting from his wisdom. Lee was also the man that differentiated between the "Asian Values" and "Western Values". Lee also wrote few books when he was a mentor minister to share his experiences and his views on the world. Graham Allison wrote a book with the great regard to him which entitled "Lee Kuan Yew: The Grand Master's Insights on China, the United States, and the World".

Chinese leaders from Deng Xiaoping to the present president Xi Jinping have learned from Lee. Xi regards him as "our senior who has our respect". Lee also shared with Deng about "open the door to the world for foreign investment". Through his visits, dialogues with Chinese leaders from the top to down, and observations, Lee could be the best man who understood China's nature of strategic calculations.

Lee said that "China has the intention to be the greatest power from the number # 1 in Asia and in the world when the time come and power grow, because it has the culture of over 4000 years old, 1.3 billion population, many of great talent-a huge and very talented pool to draw from, and "China wants to share the so co-equal to the United States". But he also argued that China "does not hurry to replace US" "it needs time to growth" "build up to catch up or overtake" and "does not want to bear burden and confront the US" and "China wants to be China and accepted as such, not as an honorary member of the West".

2.3.3.1 China Needs the National Interest, Not Changing the Global Order

The Global order has enough experiences and capacities as well as the undeniable principles to maintain itself and against the aggressors. The world order that designed by the US is easy to cooperate and make benefit, but it is hard to challenge. Historically, US observed and learned from the various previous international orders, the strengths and weakness, the values and the theory of international relations as well as the flaws of the major European major powers.

The International theory that based on interest and power, colonization, exploitation, invasion, secret diplomacy, and allied security was changed to the self-determination, decolonization, opened diplomacy, collective security, and respect of sovereignty and mutual interest. Under Wilson,

America envisioned to lead the world by these principles and called for unitedness to against the aggressors. It was the vision of the "world conscience" "Manifest destination" and "acting for mankind not self-interest". And it was the well-designed system. It has experiences to defeat the Europe, Soviet, Japan, and Germany principally, militarily, economically, politically, and diplomatically. The Chinese leaders have aware about these and know that only entering to the system that China can develop herself to become the global power and share her ideas to shape the world. Chinese leaders are clear that what they need is a stronger, powerful and prosperous nation, not the confrontation.

Lee Kuan Yew said "China is acting purely on her national interest. China does not want to challenge the existing word order". Lee gave the example of Japan and Germany that "their mistake is challenging the existing system". He continued "Chinese leaders are not stupid; they have to avoid this mistake". He added that China understands that "its fastest growth relies on the imports, including energy, raw materials, and opens the see lanes." China is the world largest trading nation, and super consumer market, and the world largest of exporting the goods. Therefore, China not only challenge to the global order, but to help maintaining and extending and opening itself wider to the globalization.

Chinese President declared that "China is always the builder of world peace, the upholder of global order, and the contributor of world economic growth". He even calls for building the "world community of shared future". But it does not mean that the existing world order is perfect without any mistake. China also can share her ideas, resources, and supporting to reshape or reform the world to spreading her influence and power gradually. Xi Jinping called "for all rounded development" and win-win cooperation, respect of mutual interest and sovereignty, and equality of all nations.

2.3.3.2 China Wants to be Number#1 in Asia and then in the World

Historically, China was the preeminent state that regarded herself in the valuable and superior position. How does history influence Chinese thought and behavior today? Answered by Michael D. Swaine, there are three attitudes: national pride alongside a strong fear of chaos; an inculcated image of a peace-loving and defensive polity alongside a strong and virtuous central government; and a unique, hierarchical yet mutually beneficial view of inter-state relations. Therefore, China is really seriously wanted to be the most powerful and respected. When Granham Alison asked "Are Chinese leaders seriously about displacing US as the number one in Asia and in the world?"", Lee Kuan Yew replied "of course. Why not? They have transformed a poor society by an economic miracle to become now the second-largest economy in the world…. There is a culture of four thousand years old with 1.3 billion people, with a huge and very talented pool to draw from. How could they not aspire to be number one in Asia, and in time the world? Every Chinese wants a strong and rich China, a nation as prosperous, advanced, and technologically competent as America, Europe, and Japan. This reawakened sense of destiny is an overpowering force.

2.3.3.3 China is Sucking the Southeast Asian Countries into Its Influence of economic system

Strategically, China needs to prepare its strategic analysis of Game Go to encircle and influence the world without using the force. The influence has to grow gradually as it sees fit and possible. China has to suck the regions by regions because its capacity and power to manage. There are also many debates about China Debt Trap in which argue that China is using the money to control those countries. Lee Kuan Yew also believed that: a) China will show those countries that China's rise is inevitable, and It would call those countries to grow together, b) China is sucking the Southeast Asia, include Japan and South Korea into its vast market and purchasing power, c) China can impose economic sanctions by denying access to its market, d) China focuses on economy and diplomacy to spread its influences.

2.3.3.4 China Needs Time to Grow, Develop the Capacity and Get Access to the Energy

Lee Kuan Yew observe deep insight into Chinese affairs, and interpreted Chinese actions which is turned back to Deng Xiaoping's advices, "observe calmly...handle our affair carefully, and bide our time". Lee argued that China needs 30 to 40 or maybe 50 years of peace and quiet rise in order to: a) catch up US, Japan, and EU, b) and to build up the market system, c) educate their children to the higher and advanced competitive skill, c) cooperate internationally for accessing to resources and energy, and e) China does not want to carry heavy burden. Lee argued that Chinese leaders know that the Economic growth is based on these factors. He said "To become competitive, China is focused on educating its young people, selecting the brightest for science and technology, followed by economics, business management, and the English language". China need time to upgrade the more capital and skill intensive to attract new investment. China needs manufacturing and industry to provide the job because the logistics and services cannot give the number of job to such a population. China will have to find out who are willing to come and invest and bring in the skills and technology to China. Besides, human resources, technology, and upgrade its system, China also needs to cooperate deeply in international and regional arena to grab the huge natural resources and energies to support its economy. Lee said "China should be given every incentive to choose international cooperation, which will absorb its energies constructively for another 50 to 100 years. This means China must have the economic opportunities to do this peacefully, without having to push its way around to get resources like oil, and have access to markets for its goods and services. If such a route is not open to China, the world must live with a pushy China".

2.3.3.5 China Needs Stability and Cooperation to Grow, not Confrontation

The Chinese grand strategy was designed with the maturity, farsightedness, and more awareness that it is called "Comprehensive National Power". It means that what the Chinese leaders want is a stronger, prosperous, civilized and cultural advancement, advanced technology and science, and modernizes the every factor of power. In short, it is a stronger and powerful China in all dimensions. China has to redefine its ways and national interests. Therefore, China needs the stability and cooperation regionally and internationally to take the opportunity to learn from others and organize itself. The confrontation and instability will ruin China's opportunity of development. There are many risk factors that determine the China National interest such internal demonstration of Xinjiang, Tibet, Hong Kong, and Taiwan, and the instability of its enamoring countries as well as the confrontation with US and its alliances. In 1989, there was an interruption to its reform and opening up of Tiananmen Square that China said that the event was "initiated by others". There have been also the American interventions and wars near Chinese borders that

China regards as the "attempt to interrupt its growth". Therefore, "China has to show its willingness to cooperate and keep its head down and smile for 40 to 50 years", Lee said. China needs peaceful rise. Lee continued "The Chinese have concluded that their best strategy is to build a strong and prosperous future, and use their huge and increasingly highly skilled and educated workers to out-sell and out-build all others. They will avoid any action that will sour up relations with the US. To challenge a stronger and technologically superior power like the US will abort their 'peaceful rise. There will be a struggle for influence. I think it will be subdued because the Chinese need the United States, need U.S. markets, U.S. technology, need to have students going to the United States to study the ways and means of doing business so they can improve their lot. It will take them 10, 20, 30 years. If you quarrel with the United States and become bitter enemies, all that information and those technological capabilities will be cut off. The struggle between the two countries will be maintained at the level that allows them to still tap the United States. China knows that it needs access to US markets, US technology, opportunities for Chinese students to study in the US and bring back to China new ideas about new frontiers. It therefore sees no profit in confronting the US in the next 20 to 30 years in a way that could jeopardize these benefits".

2.3.3.6 The Chinese Overpowering Force: Reawakening

Every Chinese leader is proud of their people because of their talents, persistence, and braveness. As president Xi Jingping said "The Chinese people are the great people; they are industrious and brave, and they never pause in pursuit of progress". It is said that "Chinese are smart, brave, persistent, hard work, ambitious, productive, but difficult to trust and low morality". Lee also admired Chinese for their endurance and self-mastering. Historically, Chinese overcame every problems and struggled to survive by themselves under many and heavy wars and natural disasters without the care from government. The hard conditions made Chinese more self-determination and hard work, and more saving. Lee saw the very special force of Chinese both people and leader who want a stronger and powerful China. Lee said "The Chinese people have raised their expectations and aspirations. Every Chinese wants a strong and rich China, a nation as prosperous, advanced, and technologically competent as America, Europe, and Japan. This reawakened sense of destiny is an overpowering force". He called the special force as "Reawakening and overpowering".

2.3.3.7 China Copies Singaporean Model of Development

There was a great emperor who made a great history of Japan was Meiji. Meiji was a great time of Japanese revolutions and transformation. His main idea was to "seek knowledge everywhere to empower the empire and change what were useless to be the useful". He opened Japan to the world by sending his ministers and students to learn everywhere and every skill, technology, military, philosophy, economy, industries, and the model of development from the west. It was the idea that what the modern society can do, Japan must catch up. Internally, he tried to reforms the traditional and outdated system, passive ideas, and he hired experts from the foreign countries to teach his people. Japan became the great power that was able to modernize and catch up the West and US, and many things were dramatically changed. Now, let's turn to the history of Singaporean development. Lee Kuan yew also opened his countries to the foreign investment, sent the minister and student to learn abroad, bringing in the skill and technology, focused on capacity and disciplinary of minister and people, and made Singapore to be the international financial and technological hub. Lee also admired Deng Xiaoping as a great and genuine leader. Lee said Deng went to visit him and discussed about the matter of development and Deng did what he told. He said to a public forum "China bring all the markets and let them compete among themselves, which require to use Chinese workers, Chinese engineer, Chinese manager, at the end, they can do final product over time. Every Moto-manufacturing cooperation in the world is in China, whether alone or joint adventure, and they have to employ Chinese. Open up, I learn from you, I catch up, I innovate, and then I compete with you". Lee said Deng went down to the major cities and said "Learn from abroad, but most of all, learn from Singapore, because it got a good system, good discipline, and do it better than them".

2.3.3.8 A Unified China is Inevitable

In order to become a real powerful China, it needs to unify Taiwan. Historically, Taiwan was the main strategic and geopolitical challenges to China that is used by others. It is the main advantaged position of chessboard of Japan and US to disturb and contain China's rise and power. As political philosophy says "the real power has no vacuum". If China does not take Taiwan, the others will use it as the threat to China, and the China's power still under the containment. As the power of China is growing with the 1.3 billion people, the small island of Taiwan has no influence to contain China. Lee said the unified China is only the matter of time. "Even though China going to use the force, there will no American intervention. Now America can intervention because Chinese Navy is still low. But next time, next time, and next time, Chinese Navy will grow more and more. For China, Taiwan is a core issues, but Taiwan is peripheral issues for US. If America goes to beat China, first time, China will come back, second time, and third time, they still come back until they win. But I think China will not use force because the economic power will resolve the two problems of independence or intervention".

2.3.3.9 China Wants to be a Global Power, not an Honorary Member of the West

Every country and every people want to be powerful, respected, recognized, and prestigious. But it depends on the capacity and conditions of how they do it. These are the main factors of Chinese ambition to be the global leader such the historical, cultural and political idea of China as the Middle

Kingdom and its prestige of wisdom and splendid in the past, the painful of humiliation period, and its 1.3 billion of human capital as well as the sense of pursuing progress. When Lee was asked "will China accept its place within the postwar order that was created by the US? Lee replied "No. It is China's intention to become the greatest power in the world—and to be accepted as China, not as an honorary member of the West". It is clear that China is now working in the international system that is designed by the US, but China needs the equal position to share her ideas, and reform the world order. Lee said "Unlike other emergent countries, China wants to be China and accepted as such, not as an honorary member of the West. The Chinese will want to share this century as co-equals with the United States. China is an old civilization and will not easily change because of external pressure or sanctions. But changes will come when their leaders, thinkers, and intellectuals become convinced on their own that adopting certain attributes and features of other societies will benefit China". China is always uphold her stand, political ideas of Marxism, the pragmatism of economic method, and alongside with her concept of virtuous or humane authority. Lee even went on to warn that "The other problem is a more crucial one: if you start off with the belief that the world has been unkind to you, the world has exploited you, the imperialists have devastated you, looted Beijing, done all this to you -- this is not good.".

2.3.3.10 Corruption, Language and Cultural Norms are the Big Challenges

There has never been a global power that has many challenges such as China today. Unlike US that geopolitically, economically, politically, technologically, intelligently, and historically give it the most satisfactory and highest positions, China is almost all weeks. America considers itself as "chosen by God, commissioned by history to play unique hegemonic role", because of these magnitudes. America works systematically under the legal training and criteria. For China, it is the mandates of heaven, but has to be achieved by supreme art of war. It means that China has to work hard, persistent, and wisely under the "Great Harmony under the Heaven". Geopolitically, China is being threatened and unsecured by internal struggling for independent declaration such as Tibet, Taiwan, Xinjiang, as well as Hong Kong who prefers the western system, and external threats and insecurity. China is surrounded by the historical enemies, strategic struggling for domination such as US, India, Japan, Vietnam, and US's allies and so on. Its neighboring countries' instability is also another challenge for China. China calls "disadvantaged position". I am going to detail all these factors in the next Chapter. I would like to point here only three challenges that mentioned by Lee Kuan Yew on the potential challenges to China's growth, the first biggest threat is "corruption" which is the biggest challenge to the communist party, the second biggest threat is the social gab and income inequality which is the most biggest threat to social division and unhappiness, and the third biggest challenge is the language and cultural norms which is the biggest threat to its capacity of innovation and growth. Lee said "China's] creativity may never match America's, because its culture does not permit a free exchange and contest of ideas". Therefore, in the report to the national congress, president Xi Jinping focused the most are "anti-corruption campaign", " the innovation, innovation, and innovation for healthy growth and core of development", and " common development". One of his great plans is to eradicate the poverty by building the human capacity and encourage them to be "a bigger ambitious".

2.3.4 Zbigniew Brzezinski's Interpretation of China's Strategic Intentions

Zbigniew Brzezinski was one of the American prominent diplomats and political thinkers. He was a Polish-American diplomat who served as the counselor of President Johnson and as the national security advisor of President Jimmy Carter. He was a very expert in international relations theory and geopolitics. Zbigniew Brzezinski forged the idea that United States and China should take the lead together to solve the global issues. In the cold war, he believed that US and China should normalize the relations and against the Soviet Unions. Zbigniew Brzezinski believed that US should strengthen the cooperation in the post-cold war order to create the better environment of global issues. He was one of the most important diplomats who knew China well and had negotiated with Chinese leaders and observed China carefully. Zbigniew Brzezinski wrote the very important books on the global politics and issues whose ideas are best to looking for. He also was one of the most important scholars.

2.3.4.1 China's Strategic Intentions

Zbigniew Brzezinski believed that China and US are both important. They both can benefit if they work out well, and they will lose both if they does not. He understood clearly that the US and China have some anxieties and suspicions. For US, the anxiety is China takes advantages on its economy and technology. For China, America takes advantages on its internal affairs, organizes the coalitions against China. He also warned that the both sides are carefully observed and analyzed others' actions and prepared to respond accordingly. Brzezinski also believed that China is surrounded by uncomfortable and anxious geopolitics, the US, Japan, India, Vietnam and internal challenges. Observed China' actions carefully, he wrote in his famous book "strategic vision: America and crisis of global power" as China is struggling to handle these difficulties and wish to become the global power are driving by six major objectives:

1. To reduce the dangers inherent in China's potential geographical encirclement, due to: the US security links with Japan, South Korea, and the Philippines; the vulnerability to interdiction of China's maritime access into the Indian Ocean through the Strait of Malacca and thence to the Middle East, Africa, Europe, and so on; and the absence of available Economically sustainable land routes for trade with Europe through the vast distances of Russia and Central Asia;

2. To establish for itself a favored position in an emerging East Asian community (which could include a China-Japan-South Korea free trade zone) and likewise in the already-existing ASEAN, while containing—though not yet excluding—a major US presence or role in them;

3. To consolidate Pakistan as a counterweight to India and to gain through it a more proximate and safer access to the Arabian Sea and the Persian Gulf;

4. To gain a significant edge over Russia in economic influence in Central Asia and Mongolia, thereby satisfying in part China's needs for natural resources also in areas closer to China than Africa or Latin America;

5. To resolve in China's favor the remaining unsettled legacy of its civil war Taiwan—in keeping with Deng's formula (first enunciated publicly to the Chinese media in the course of a visit to him by this writer) of "one China, two systems";

6. To establish for itself a favored economic, and indirectly political, presence in a number of Middle Eastern, African, and Latin American countries, thereby securing stable access to raw materials, minerals, agricultural products, and energy—while simultaneously securing a dominant position in

local markets for China's competitively priced manufactured products, and, in the process, thereby gaining a global political constituency on China's behalf.

2.3.5 China's World Order and Its Challenges

There are three the political values that are being practiced in China, the Marxism, the economic pragmatism, and Chinese traditional values. These ideas and the mixing of Chinese great history of preeminence in the past, the lessons from the evolution of global conditions as well as learning from the modern societies, has been paving the way for Chinese prosperity. China wants to be the global power with its ideas and system, but there are many challenges.

China's concept of world order has its root in economy, moral philosophy, and humane authority which practice in the practical and conceptual ways of the philosophy of its ancient sages and strategists and the mixing with Marxism. China will spread its influence gradually through its economic power and magnitude of culture. China wants to regain its past preeminent position that it used to have. As mentioned by Lee Kuan Yew China wants to replace US in Asia and as well as in the world. The points to mention in this Chapter are: Chinese cultural influences, Chinese philosophies of order, and Chinese political system.

2.3.5.1 Chinese Historical and Cultural Influences

The Chinese culture has been progressed and developed over 5000 years ago. It has the great moral sense that plays very important roles in building the social progress, the social harmony that the world has to learn from China. The written Chinese Characters that are being used now were created during the Shang Dynasty in the second millennium B.C. The people still can read the letter that written during the Confucian era. The famous ancient Chinese philosophers, socialist, psychologist, strategist…ideas has been rooted profoundly in Chinese society and has been spreading to the world. The brilliant insight of Lao Zi, Confucius, Mencius, Zhuang Zi and many other ancient sages has been passed down on. Chinese cultural and leadership styles had extended in the size much larger than any of Europe's.

"At its ultimate extent, the Chinese cultural sphere stretched over a continental area much larger than any European state, indeed about the size of continental Europe. Chinese language and culture, and the Emperor's political writ, expanded to every known terrain: from the steppe lands and pine forests in the north shading into Siberia, to the tropical jungles and terraced rice farms in the south; from the east coast with its canals, ports, and fishing villages, to the stark deserts of Central Asia and the ice-capped peaks of the Himalayan frontier. The extent and variety of this territory bolstered the sense that China was a world unto itself. It supported a conception of the Emperor as a figure of universal consequence, presiding over tian xia, or "All Under Heaven."

The Chinese values have been influenced over Asia the very long time ago, and not only the political system, but also the social and in the mindset of people. Chinese leaders used to think that the surrounding people and the countries were the vassals and belonged to Chinese. During the Mao's revolutions and changed the country to Communism, a new China, the words "overseas Chinese" was used. The thought of Chairman Moa was brought to the overseas Chinese. They used the words overseas Chinese because in their mind all the people who went to other places and states around its borders were originated from China. That why China regards itself as the middle kingdom. The overseas Chinese could go their homeland without Visa until 1969. Zhou Enlai in order to prevent the overseas Chinese from thinking of going home and gave the right to the country where Chinese lived said the term " overseas Chinese" is not accurate as many had taken up citizenship of their countries residences. Even though the Chinese leaders stop recognizing overseas Chinese, the cultural influences that it has made many people even not a Chinese regard themselves as Chinese if they are cute and white, clever and rich. Nowadays, the Chinese language and culture are being spread to the part of the world through institute Confucius and its economic power.

2.3.5.2 Chinese Concepts of Order

There were many prominent philosophers and strategists that their insights shape the Chinese concept of world and domestic order. The Chinese concepts of order are based on the philosophies of Confucius, Mozi, the Art of War by Sun Tzu, and the legalism. These concepts are based on the high morality and the responsibility, the economic growth, the enforcement of the law, and the power of military.

Confucius believed that when the people are highly behaved and honest to their duties are the main principles of harmony and order. He said "when the leaders are being the leaders, the ministers are being minister, and father is being the father, the sons are being the sons; the society and world will be in harmony and order". His principle of five relationships is the center of peace, order, harmony and prosperity. They are: leader and ministers, the parents and children, the husband and wife, the elder brother and younger brother, and the friendship. Confucius believed that the leader is the superior man that sent by the heaven to create the harmony on earth. Therefore, the leader must be a virtuous, wise and faithful. The leader sets the good example for his ministers and people. The people will benefit from the wisdom and the virtue of the leader. For the ministers, they are in the middle of the leader and the people. So, they have to be honest to both the leader and people. They have to be honest to their obligations and perform their duties well. For the people, Confucius focused on the proper behavior and good heart. This is what China now called "Humane Authority".

Contrast to Confucianism who focuses on the morality and the willingness of the leader and the people, the legalism believes on the tough punishment and the enforcement of the law. This school of thought believes that the nature of human is cruel, deceptive, untruthful, selfish, and disordered. In order to suppress these natures and put the people back to the order, the punishment and the law enforcement are needed. This school of thought attained its preeminence at the time of Warring States. This school of thought criticized the Confucianism whom believes in the virtue of the leader and morality of the people. The philosophers in this school were Shang Yang, Hanfeizi, and Li Si. They believed that "if the evil minister enjoys safety and profit, it is the begging of downfall. The tough law enforcement makes the strong country". The law is superior to all the people.

The philosopher whose ideas were similar to Confucius' was Mozi. Mozi believed in three ways of the order. The first is the virtuous and learned ministers. He said "if the scholars are not protected and used, that state will be in declination. Therefore, the plan for the country has to be shared only with the scholars". The second, he believed that the world order is based on the universal love and compassion. He said "If everyone in the world will love universally; states not attacking one another; houses not disturbing one another; thieves and robbers becoming extinct; emperor and ministers, fathers and sons, all being affectionate and filial — if all this comes to pass the world will be orderly. Therefore, how can the wise man that has charge of governing the empire fail to restrain hate and encourage love? So, when there is universal love in the world it will be orderly, and when there is mutual hate in the world it will be disorderly". Third, he believed that "the poverty is the root of chaos and disorder". Deng Xiaoping also said that "to be rich is glorious". And the modern China is being built on the concept that "as long as the economic growth continuously, the people will tolerate with many things". Deng Xiaoping once said "the military can end the unrest, but the economy can prevent it in the future".

2.3.5.3 Chinese Political System

There are three Chinese political ideas that is being practiced in Beijing, the Maxims with the Chinese characteristics, the pragmatism of economy, and Chinese traditional values.

Two systems, one country is the People's Republic of China. While the liberalism seems declining, China can use these concepts with its traditional values such as fairness, righteousness, humane authority, and the mixing with the liberalist values and so on to influence and impress the world.

The communism which originated in Soviet Union and then spread to the world, now, it does no longer exist in its birth-country, but in China, the world largest communist country. To the Chinese leaders, only socialism with Chinese characteristics can China survive and strong. The system has its theory, path and principles. So, socialism with Chinese characteristics is the core value that all Chinese leaders have to uphold and emphasize. China realizes its prosperity and stands firm in the international stage with in prestige is because they follow the socialism with the Chinese Characteristics. It is the fundamental achievements.

"Only by upholding the Socialism with Chinese characteristics can we bring together and lead the whole party, the whole nation and the people of all ethnic groups in realizing a moderately prosperous society by the centenary of CPC in 2021 and in turning China to a prosperous, democratic, culturally advanced and harmonious modern socialist country by the centenary of People's Republic of China in 2049, so as to ensure the people greater happiness and the nation a brighter future."

Since the early 20th century, It experienced three revolutions and had has the very bitter history of bloodshed and hardship, the collapse of Qing Dynasty in 1911, Mao shifting to Communism in 1949, and the Deng' era of opening up and reform in 1977. They always think about the long-term strategy and steps and stages in what and when should be done. In Mao' era was the time of fighting to gain independence, unify and building the communist country, in Deng Xiaoping, it was the time of reform and opening up the china to the world. Jiang Zemin, strengthen the moral values of the Chinese people. Ho Jintao expanded the Chinese economic development to the outside world, and Xi Jinping is the time to summing up and strengthening the system. Deng, who started to open up and reform China, knew that Chinese people lived in poverty, famine, wars, natural disaster and under the controlling of other nations in the very long time. Lives were hard, difficult, painful and exhausted. So, he picked up the vision of building the economic power in which means that the Chinese will have the good basic needs, live in peace and prosperity. Contrast to Mao who focused on ideology, Deng focused on economic development, Moa played the competitive strategy, Deng built up and normalized the relations with other countries. That's why the words that often used by Deng were "Open your mind, free your mind or emancipate your mind." Then the two systems, one country, and the Socialism with the Chinese Characteristic were built up during his period.

Now, China realizes its prosperity as the world largest economic power, the richest nation from the poorest in the1950s, from the nation that used to be deprived, looked down to the nation that is honored and respected with its values, economic and military power. Moreover, China now possesses the four major potentials, largest population, largest economic power, the third of most powerful military might, and diplomatic power. China practices both of the economic models are the state and private enterprises. The idea was initiated by Deng Xiaoping. It has made China gain its very fast growth over these four decades. In easy word to say is "Chinese government doesn't depend only on taxation but it does the business by itself, as well as allows the private company to invest". And for the Chinese traditional values are can be found in the mixing philosophies of Confucius, Mozi, Shang Yang and Hanfei zi so on. China will use the system to image itself as the global power.

2.3.5.4 The Challenges of Chinese and American Concepts of World Order

The Sino-US relations are the most important of world peace, prosperity and growth. Both countries have the common and competitive interests. Their concepts of World Order, Values, Systems, Visions and Emotions are different. Both countries feel uncomfortable to each other. And both strategic thinkers are looking for the reasonable proclamations to show the wrongness of each other. The challenges also go through the competitive position as the Ancient Creek philosopher, Thucydides, mentioned the "Trap of Power".

The America and China have their own values and systems. To America, its values and political systems serve as the best and the universal ones which are applicable to every nation in the world. Without these qualities, the world will not be stable, prosperous, and peaceful. The people will be suffered owing to the political suppression. American leaders support the citizen in the world to fight for freedom, democracy, and liberty as its core values. America's version, though more recent and more nuanced, is also somewhat self-centered — a moral order where everything will be fine once the world comes to its senses and thinks like America. American leaders like imposing their values and giving its democratic lessons to the world in which these things are the most disliked by

Chinese leaders. To Chinese leaders, China does not need the American values, system or democratic lessons. There is no model of leadership that can be applied to all nations. Every nation has its values, characteristics, traditions, feelings, and emotions so on. A very good system in one country does not mean it is also good for others. For China, the only Socialism with Chinese Characteristics that is applicable and inspired by Chinese people. China has enough experiences, leadership styles, and values. The Chinese exceptionalism is its cultural magnitudes, whereas American exceptionalism is democracy.

The China and America also feel very uncomfortable to each other. Philosophy says that "the root of conflict is the unhappy emotions that bear in mind". Both countries are looking at other's activities carefully and responding accordingly. America feels bad of China because it thinks that China is playing unfair trade, doing the business with the dictators, abusing the intellectual property, abusing the human right, and taking the advantages of American technology and economy. For China, America is the trouble-makers for China and other nations, uses the human right as the business, tries to contain and prevent China from growing, tries to seize China, and interfere in Chinese internal affair. However, both sides know that US-China relations are very important for world peace and prosperity. America needs Chinese market, cheap goods, and money, while China also needs the US's investment and technologies.

The US-China relations are not different from US-Russia relations during the World Wars. During the cold war, China was a US partner in confronting the USSR threat. When Vietnam invaded Cambodia in 1979 in the purpose of building Indochina, China under Deng understood that this would be very dangerous for China in future. He went to normalize the relationship with US then to many countries in Asia to gain the legal right to fight Vietnam and force it to withdraw its military from Cambodia in 1989. However, when the Cold War was over, America knew that China will be the potential opponent of US. China will become the most powerful nation in Asia and in the world. In Bush administration, there were the two opinions about American foreign policy toward China: one, favored by Bush, to encourage gradual change through the process of constructive engagement, and other favored by Congress to impose sanctions and apply political and economic pressure for human rights and political reform. Since the terrorist attacked of 11 September, America under Bush leadership used this reason to invade Afghanistan by cooperated with Pakistan which is very close to the Chinese border and built up its military bases in central Asia, the resourceful places. US even strengthened the US-Japanese relations, and solved the weapons to Taiwan, allowed Taiwanese president to visit the US. Taiwan is the part of US's game in bargaining with China. The American ambition is still enrooted deeply in Asia as the whole that is the great obstacle of China to become the superpower. The military exercises between US and its alliances are made every year particularly. In addition, the ongoing problem that both countries disagree over the North Korean Nuclear, South China Sea, World Economic Order, and so on.

The another biggest challenge is about the struggling to gain the position as the global power by China, and about struggling to beat and contain China by America. There was an ancient creek philosopher and historian who wrote that "It was the rise of Athens, and the fear this inspired in Sparta that made the war inevitable". Therefore, it is the rise of China to be the global power, and it is the fear of the United States of losing its dominant position that is making the trade war inevitable". The philosophy says "if you are able to beat your enemy down. You have to beat before it become too late. When your opponent reaches your level it is too late. You cannot ask for the mercy from your enemy, but you have to be stronger to force him to the order". This is what American strategic thinkers believe. Both American and Chinese thinkers believe that China will overtake the US. Therefore, before China reaching the advantaged position, US thinkers concluded that "China has to be beaten and contained".

No one knows what the China will do if it will become the superpower and replace the US. And the US itself does not know how it will be treated. Will China be more aggressive and assertive? So, thinking in the long term and consequence, China cannot be allowed to reach such a position. The Trump's administration concluded that "America has to be stronger, and China has to be beaten and contained. Only when you are stronger that you can make sure that your interest can be protected, and you will know surely how the world will work". Historically and presently, there have been two strategic thinkings of US "beat others by one hand, develop yourself by one hand". To contain and beat China, US has to gather the Chinese opponents to work together.

China knows that it has the long way to go. It needs to develop the human capacity and depend on US technology to maintain the economic growth. China may think in these ways "We want to bid the time and grow up. But we are being beaten and contained. The nature of our enemy is making us the problems, encircle and interrupt our growth. In the recent history, we beard the very heavy burden, we are humiliated, invaded, interfered, but we were able to deal with. Now, they are afraid of our growth, and then gather against us. If we fight back we will lose. Therefore, we have to down our face and smile gently. We have to seek for the relative advantages". The relative advantage is the soft power that China has to seek for cooperation internationally.

The middle kingdom who gives much value on economic development will compete the US in seeking for natural resources everywhere and improve the diplomacy with every country for the good of economic progress. In Asia as the whole, Europe, Africa, Australia, and South America will become the main Chinese economic partners. For its national interest, China does not want to interfere in others' internal affair. It focuses only on the economic ties because it determines the destiny of Communist party. Many international or regional trade organizations have the presence of China, and it plays crucial roles ever. On one hand, China has to adapt itself into international law and conducted reform. During the period of transformation, China will bear many burdens.

2.3.5.5 The Scholars' words about China

- During the long process of history, by relying on our own diligence, courage and wisdom, Chinese people have opened up a good and beautiful home where all ethnic groups live in harmony and fostered an excellent culture that never fades. (Xi Jinping).

-We want to learn from the west about science and technology and how to manage the economy, but this must be combined with specific conditions here. That's how we have made great progress in the last twenty years. (Zemin Jiang).

-The problem for China is political. China is held together by money, not ideology. When there is an economic downturn and the money stops rolling in, not only will the banking system spasm, but the entire fabric of Chinese society will shudder. Loyalty in China is either bought or coerced. Without available money, only coercion remains. Business slowdowns can generally lead to instability because they lead to business failure and unemployment. In a country where poverty is endemic and unemployment widespread, the added pressure of an economic downturn will result in political instability. (George Friedman).

Bibliography

I. Primary Resources

Kissinger, Henry. *World order*. New York: The Penguin Press, 2014.

Kissinger, Henry. *Diplomacy*. Simon & Schuster, 1994.

Kissinger, Henry. *On China*. New York: The Penguin Press, 2011.

Ferguson, Niall. *Kissinger. The idealist*. New York: Penguin Books.

Charles Hauss. *Beyond Confrontation: Transforming the New World Order.*

Praeger 1996

Shogo Suzuki. *International Orders in the Early Modern World: Before the Rise of the*

West. Routledge, 2013.

Kenneth Surin, *Freedom Not Yet Liberation and the Next World Order.* Duke

University: Press Books, 2009.

Paul Joseph Watson. *Order Out of Chaos (Elite Sponsored Terrorism & the New World*

Order). Alex Jones Productions, 2003.

A. Ralph Epperson, *New World Order*. Publius Press, 1990.

Alex Jones. *9-11 descent into tyranny-the New World Order's dark plans to turn Earth into a prison planet*. AEJ Pub, 2002.

Michael Skinner. *American Imperialism-The New World Order and its Systematic*

*Ideology of Wa*r, York University, 2007.

David Allen Rivera. *Final Warning - History of the New World Order-Progressive.*

Press (1997)

F William Engdahl. *Full Spectrum Dominance-Totalitarian Democracy in the New*

World Order. Createspace ,2009.

F. William Engdahl. *A Century of War-Anglo-American Oil Politics and the New World Order*. Pluto Press :2004.

David Allen- *FINAL-WARNING-A-History-of-the-New-World-Order*. 2004.

Garry Leech.*Crude Interventions-The United States, Oil and the New World (Dis) Order*. Zed Books: 2006.

Henry Kissinger. *The Establishment Of A New World Order,* 2014

HG Wells - *The New World Order.* 1940.

Jasper. Global Tyranny Step-By-Step: The-United Nations and the Emerging New

World Order. 1992.

Javaid Rehman. *Islamic State Practices, International Law and the Threat from Terrorism-a Critique Of The 'clash Of Civilizations' In the New World Order.*2005

John C. Hulsman. *A Paradigm for the New World Order_ Schools-of-Thought Analysis of American Foreign Policy in the Post-Cold War Era.* Palgrave Macmillan, 1997.

Markus Kaim. *Great Powers and Regional Orders (Us Foreign Policy and Conflict in The Islamic World).* 2008.

Parag Khanna. *The Second World-Empires and Influence in the New Global Order.*

Random House, 2008.

Samuel P. Huntington. *The Clash of Civilizations and the Remaking of World Order*.

Simon & Schuster,1996.

Mohammad Ali. *The New World Order – Islamic*. Lahore, 1944.

Thomas Volgy, *Mapping the New World Order*. Wiley-Blackwell, 2009.

William R. Nester. *American Power, the New World Order and the Japanese Challenge*. Palgrave Macmillan, 1992.

Bruce W, Jentleson. *American Foreign Policy,* USA, 2014

Brian D. Taylor. *State Building in Putin's Russia,* Syracuse Uni. 2011.

Richard Sakwa. *Putin and the Oligarchs*, I.B.Tauris & Co. Ltd, 2014.

Marcel H. Herpen. *Putin's Wars:The Rise of Russia's New Imperialism,* Rowman, 2014

A. Ralph Epperson, "New *World Order*", Publius Press, 1990.

Joel Colton, *A History of the modern World,* Knopf: 2001.

Phill Williams, *Superpower competition and crisis prevention in third world.* Cam.Uni press, 2009.

Ian Adams. *Fifty Major Political Thinkers.* Routledge Key Guides 2nd Edition: 2007.

Michael D. Barr. *Lee Kuan Yew and the "Asian Values".* 2007

Markus Kaim, *Great Powers and Regional Orders: Us Foreign Policy and Conflict in the Islamic World.* Ashgate, USA: 2008.

James Stewart Martin. *All Honorable Men: New World Order and the rise of Hitler*, Annapolis: 1950.

Hugh Kennedy, *The Great Arab Conquests- How the Spread of Islam Changed the World We Live In.* Da Capo Press, 2008.

R R Palmer, *A History of the Modern World.* , London ,Knopf: 2007

Martin Kramer , The Ideals of an Islamic order, 2014

Maulana Muhammad Ali, *The New World Order*, Lashore: 1994.

Aini Linjakumpu, *Political Islam in the Global World.* THACA: 2007.

Steve Donoghue, *America's War for the Greater Middle East' surveys decades of Failed policy.* USA: 2016.

Joachim Whaley, Germany and the Holy Roman Empire- Volume I- Maximilian I to the Peace of Westphalia. Oxford University Press: USA 2012.

Bruce W. Jentleson, *American Foreign Policy*. Duke Uni. USA: 2014

Friedman. George. *The Next 100 Years, A Forecast For The Twenty-First Century*. Doubleday: 2009.

James Wilson, *American Government Institutions and Policies*. Gengage learning,
14th edition: 2015.

Paul Kelly. *The Politics Book (Big Ideas Simply Explained)*. DK Publishing, USA: 2013

Da vid McKay. *American Politics and Society*. Wiley Blackwell: 2013.

Roger Leroy Mill. *NTC's American government*. McGraw-Hill: 2006.

Zbigniew Brzezinski. *The Grand Chessboard: American Primacy and Its Geostrategic Imperatives*. Basic books: 1997.

Robert S. Rush, *GI The US Infantryman in World War II*. Osprey Publishing:2003. William E. Burns. *Speeches in world history*. Literary Collections: 2010.

Brad Roberts. *Weapons Proliferation and World Order: After the Cold War.* (Martinus Nijhoff: 1996

William J. Clinton, Public Papers of the Presidents of the United States, (Government Printing Office: 2000.

Mart Laita, Created Equal, (Steidl Photography International: 2009), p 01.

Gordon Williamson. *German Special Forces of World War II.* Osprey Publishing Ltd: 2009

Dr. Henry Kissinger, *Bilderberger Conference.* Evians, France: 1991.

Lee Kuan Yew, *From Third World to First.* Hamper 2000.

Anthea Roberts, *Is international Law International.* Oxford University Press: 2017.

Agnia Grigas, *Beyond Crimea: The New Russian Empire.* Yale University Press: 2016.

Xi Jinping , *The Governance of China. English Language Version.* Shanghai Press: 2015.

Marcel H. Van Herpen. Putin's Wars:The Rise of Russia's New Imperialism.Rowman: 2014.

Lampton David. *Following the Leader Ruling China, from Deng Xiaoping to XiJinping.* University of California Press: 2014.

Vogel, Ezra F. *Deng Xiaoping and the transformation of China.* Belknap Press: 2013.

Daniel M. Ingram. *Mastering the Core Teaching of the Buddha: An Unusually   Hardcore Dharma Book.* Aeon Books: 2008.

O.H. de A. Wijesekera. *The Three Signata: Anicca, Dukkha, Anatta:* The Wheel Publication No. 20, BPS: 1960.

Kunapayuta. *A pictorial biography of Sakyamuni Buddha.* In Khmer-English: 2001.

His Holiness the Dalai Lama. *The Middle Way: Faith Grounded in Reason.* Wisdom   Publications 2edition: 2014.

Geshe Tashi Tsering. *The Four Noble Truths: The Foundation of Buddhist Thought.* Wisdom Publications: 2005.

David N. Snyder, *The Complete Book of Buddha'sLists-Explained.* Vipassana Foundation: 2006.

G. P. Malalasekera, *Buddhism and the Race Question.* BPS: 1974.

Prof. Kurt Leidecker. *Buddhism and Democracy.* BPS: 2011.

G. P. Malalasekera, Buddhism and the Race Question, BPS :2006.

Bhikkhu Nyanatusita. *Analysis of the Bhikkhu Patimokkha.* BPS: 2014.

Dr. Kapila Abhayawansa. *The Global Society,* IBC: Thailand.

Santidhammo Bhikkhu. *Maha Ghosananda: The Buddah of the Battlefield.* S. R.Printing 2009.

Javad H. Kashani. *The impact of family violence on children and adolescents.* Sage Publication: 1998.

Janet Surrey.*The Buddha's Wife: The Path of Awakening Together.* Atria Books:2015.

Winitha Jinasena. *Sigalovada Sutta: (A Practical way for an Ideal Life).* Buddhist Cultural Center: 2009.

II. The Secondary Sources

theatlantic.com/international/archive/2016/11/kissinger-order-and-chaos.

Retrieved On 15 October 2016.

www.henryakissinger.com/articles.html. Retrieved on 15 October 2016.

Web Retrieved on 15   October 2016.

Youtube: China-major-diplomacy. Web. Retrieved on 28 October 2016.

on 14 November 2016.

www.bloomberg.com/view/articles/. Retrieved on 17 November 2016.

www.cia.gov/library/publications/the-world-factbook/geos/us.html.   Retrieved on 19November 2016.

Pres. George.H. W Bush, State of Union address, 04-29-1991,

en.wikipedia.org/wiki/Winston_Churchill. Web Retrieved on 24 November 2016.

Dr. Henry Kissinger, *giving interview at Chinatownhall*, Published online on 20 June,2016.

.wikipedia.org/wiki/New_world_order_ (politics). Retrieved on 29 December 2016.

en.wikipedia.org/wiki/Chinese Communist Revolution. Retrieved on 30 December2016.

www.ancient.eu/Siddhartha_Gautama/> Retrieved on 20 January 2017.

www.accesstoinsight.org/lib/authors/bodhi/waytoend.html. Retrieved 17 January 207.

en.wikipedia.org/wiki/Pratītyasamutpāda. Retrieved on 25 January 2017.